The
Pocketbook
of
Reading and Spelling Reminders

C000045755

by

Linda Riley

The Pocketbook of Reading & Spelling Reminders
by Linda Riley

ISBN 1 - 84370 - 005 0
British Library Cataloguing in Publication Data.
A catalogue record for this book is available from the British Library.

© Linda Riley 2002

Design & Editorial Philippa Chudley - Cover designed by Tom Wells Associates
Illustrated by Chris Middleton & Jade Munslow-Ong

This title is part of the MEMORY MOTIVATORS series, order code: PB 0050
Published by: **Multi-Sensory Learning Ltd**
Highgate House, Creaton, Northamptonshire, NN6 8NN, United Kingdom

About the Author:
Linda Riley B.A.(Hons.), Cert. Ed., A.M.B.D.A.

Linda Riley is a dyslexia specialist. A practising teacher and teacher-trainer, she has written learning materials for Multi-Sensory Learning since 1995. This Pocketbook originated in the need expressed by her students for a quick, handy reminder of key reading and spelling points.

Most of our language is quite logical.
Most of the words we need to spell or read are quite easy!

This Memory Motivators Pocketbook includes the **most important** reminders to make spelling and reading easier.
It starts to unlock the logic of our language.

Remember that a little book like this does not contain everything, but only the most important things.

Contents

Reminders

The Alphabet of the English Language

a b c d **e** f g

h **i** j k l m n

o p q r s t **u**

v w x y z

5 vowels
21 consonants
y is sometimes used as a vowel

Note! *The 26 letters of the alphabet combine together to stand for the 44 different sounds of the English language.*

7

A **syllable** *is a beat in a word.*

Every **syllable** *must have a* **vowel**.

f**u**n   **(1)**
f**u**nn**y**   **(2)**
f**u**nn**ily**   **(3)**

Codes used in this book.....

( )   shows the sound we hear

—   shows the vowel sound is long

◡   shows the vowel sound is short

V   means vowel

C   means consonant

/   shows syllable separation

Each **vowel** *can stand for a*

'short' sound.........

($\breve{a}$) as in **cat**

($\breve{e}$) as in **leg**

($\breve{i}$) as in **sit**

($\breve{o}$) as in **dog**

($\breve{u}$) as in **fun**

<u>or a</u>

'long' sound.........

$(\bar{a})$ as in **apron**

$(\bar{e})$ as in **secret**

$(\bar{i})$ as in **item**

$(\bar{o})$ as in **open**

$(\bar{u})$ as in **unit**

11

A **suffix**

is put on the <u>end</u> of a word to change its **use**

vowel suffix.....

ing	*jump**ing***
ed	*jump**ed***
er	*jump**er***
y	*jump**y***

consonant suffix.....

ly	*quick**ly***
ful	*hope**ful***
less	*hope**less***

A **prefix**

is put on the <u>beginning</u> of a word to change its **meaning**

un	**un***well*
im	**im***press*
dis	**dis***miss*
re	**re***fill*
de	**de***frost*

Word Patterns

Word Patterns are important!

They tell us.....

how to <u>read</u> the vowels

how many vowels to <u>write</u> in a word
how many consonants to <u>write</u> between the vowels

how long the word is likely to be

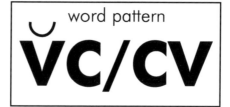

Words with this pattern have

2 syllables with 2 consonants

between the vowels.

The first vowel is 'short'.

17

magnet

mag/net

2 syllables

2 consonants together

m**a**gn**e**t

**2 vowels
1st vowel 'short'**

18

kidnap   helmet   letter

V̆C/CV

hopping

hop/ping

2 syllables

2 consonants together

h**o**pp**i**ng

2 vowels
1st vowel 'short'

tennis   contact   dinner

19

word pattern

V̄/CV

Words with this pattern have

2 syllables with 1 consonant

between the 2 vowels.

The first vowel is 'long'.

word pattern
V̄/CV

(hoping)

ho/ping
2 syllables

1 consonant
ho(p)ing
1st vowel 'long'

| pilot | hotel | rider |

22

smiling

smi/ling
2 syllables

1 consonant

smiling

1st vowel 'long'

dining	basin	open

23

word pattern

V̆C/V

24

Words with this pattern also have

2 syllables with 1 consonant

between the 2 vowels.

<u>BUT</u> the first vowel is 'short'.

robin

rob/in

2 syllables

1 consonant

robin

1st vowel 'short'

| comic | denim | timid |

26

̆VC/V

panic

pan/ic

2 syllables

1 consonant

pa(n)ic

1st vowel 'short'

| visit | topic | rapid |

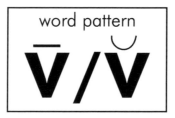

word pattern

V̄ / V̆

28

Words with this pattern have

2 syllables with no consonant

between the 2 vowels.

The first vowel is 'long'

and the second vowel is 'short'.

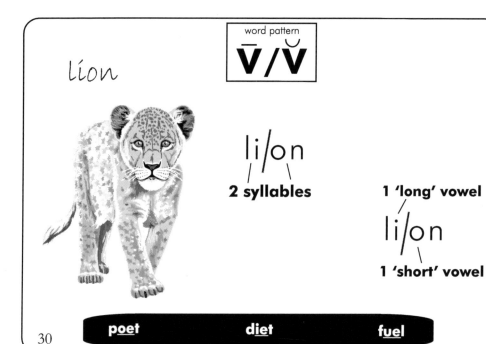

word pattern

V̄/V̆

lion

li/on
2 syllables

1 'long' vowel
li/on
1 'short' vowel

p<u>oe</u>t   d<u>ie</u>t   f<u>ue</u>l

30

fuel

f u / e l
2 syllables

1 'long' vowel
f u / e l
1 'short' vowel

d<u>ia</u>l   vid<u>eo</u>   r<u>ui</u>n

31

Spelling

Words can.....

sound **long** but look **short!**

area

3 syllables 4 letters

idea

Words can.....

sound **short** but look **long!**

straight   *1 syllable 8 letters*

through   *1 syllable 7 letters*

Words can.....

be **long** but **easy** to spell!

optimistic

uninhabited

transatlantic

electromagnetic

Words can.....

be **short** but **hard** to spell**!**

eye

half

weigh

cough

c or k ?

Use **k** if the next letter is
e
i
y

Use **c** if the next letter is anything else!

kitten	**ca**t
kept	**co**st
s**ky**	**cu**t
	crisp
	clap

k *or* ck ?

after **one short vowel** ⟶ *use* **ck**

after
a consonant
2 vowels together ⟶ *use* **k**
a long vowel

k or ck ?

b**ck** ban**k** bea**k** ba**k**e
lick lin**k** loo**k** li**k**e
t**ick**et tan**k**er soa**k**ing ta**k**en

ick *or* ic ?

use **ick**.....

at the end of a **1 syllable word**

use **ic**.....

at the end of a **word of more than 1 syllable**

ick *or* ic ?

p**ick**   br**ick**   st**ick**   qu**ick**

com**ic**   pan**ic**   traff**ic**   picn**ic**

elast**ic**   athlet**ic**   fantast**ic**

Use **ss**, **ll**, *or* **ff**

after **one short vowel**

at the end of a word.

42

$$\boxed{ss} \quad \boxed{ll} \quad \boxed{ff}$$

pre**ss**   **but**   clo**s**e   cla**s**p   nur**s**e

mi**ll**   **but**   mi**l**e   mea**l**   gir**l**

stu**ff**   **but**   li**f**e   hoo**f**   sel**f**

Use **tch** *for* (ch)

after **one short vowel**

Except:
such   **much**   **rich**   **which**   **sandwich**

tch or ch ?

pa**tch** *but* por**ch** pou**ch**

ba**tch** *but* ben**ch** bea**ch**

ti**tch** *but* tor**ch** tou**ch**

Use **dge** *for* (j)

after **one short vowel**

dge *or* ge ?

ba**dge** *but* bar**ge** pa**ge**

fri**dge** *but* frin**ge**

lo**dge** *but* loun**ge**

nu**dge** *but* hu**ge** stoo**ge**

Long Vowel Choices

apron $(\bar{a})$ secret $(\bar{e})$ item $(\bar{i})$ open $(\bar{o})$ uniform $(\bar{u})$

$(\bar{a})$

just a	D**a**vid	open syllable
a-e	g**a**m**e**	middle
ai	r**ai**n	middle
ay	pl**ay**	end

Will D**a**vid pl**ay** that g**a**m**e** in the r**ai**n?

49

just **e**	P**e**ter	open syllable
ee	gr**ee**n thr**ee**	middle end
ea	m**ea**l p**ea**	middle end
e-e	compl**ete**	end

Peter's compl**ete** m**ea**l was thr**ee** gr**ee**n p**ea**s.

$(\overline{i})$		
just i	Simon	open syllable
i-e	ri**de**	middle
igh	n**igh**t	middle
y	sk**y**	end

Simon can **ride** in the sk**y** at n**igh**t.

(ō)

just o	T**o**by	open syllable
o-e	h**o**m**e**	middle
oa	b**oa**t	middle
ow	r**ow**	end

Will T**o**by r**ow** his b**oa**t h**o**m**e**?

52

(ū)

just **u**	J**u**dy	open syllable
u-e	**u**s**e**	middle
ue	barbe**cue**	end
ew	n**ew**	end

Will J**u**dy **use** the n**ew** barbec**ue**?

53

oi or oy ?

Use **oy** *at the* **end of a word**
and also before **a vowel**

Use **oi** everywhere else!

oi or oy ?

b<u>oi</u>l   c<u>oi</u>n   n<u>oi</u>se   v<u>oi</u>ce

t<u>oi</u>let   rej<u>oi</u>ce   app<u>oi</u>nt

b<u>oy</u>   enj<u>oy</u>   empl<u>oy</u>

l<u>oy</u>al   v<u>oy</u>age   s<u>oy</u>a

ou or ow ?

Use **ow** *at the* **end** of a word
before '**n**' on its own
before '**l**'
before **a vowel**
sometimes before '**d**'

Use **ou** everywhere else!

ou or ow ?

loud   sh**ou**t   c**ou**nt
r**ou**nd   h**ou**se   b**ou**nce

h**ow**   n**ow**   all**ow**
t**ow**n   br**ow**n   cl**ow**n
h**ow**l   gr**ow**l   **ow**l
t**ow**er   v**ow**el   c**ow**ard
cr**ow**d   p**ow**der

| **t** or **ed?** |

*Use **ed** for the sound **(t)***

if the meaning is

an action that happened in the past.

t or ed?

jumped   *peeped*   *stopped*

cooked   *barked*   *packed*

wished   *missed*   *fixed*

d or ed?

*Use **ed** for the sound **(d)***

if the meaning is

an action that happened in the past.

d or ed?

bang**ed**   hugg**ed**   wav**ed**

fill**ed**   smil**ed**   rubb**ed**

humm**ed**   zoom**ed**   moan**ed**

tion, sion or cian?

*For the sound **(shun)**.......*
*use **'tion'** most of the time!*

*use **'sion'** after **'l'**, **'n'**, **'r'**, and **'s'***
*use **'cian'** for an occupation.*

tion

action   section   direction

position   ambition   superstition

option   subscription   disruption

station   relation   education

sion

emulsion   convulsion   repulsion

mansion   pension   dimension

version   excursion   diversion

passion   mission   profession

cian

opti**cian** musi**cian** magi**cian**

electri**cian** politi**cian**

mathemati**cian** statisti**cian**

le, el or al?

After a consonant, at the end of a word

Use '__le__' for the sound (l)

BUT...

If the consonant is 'm', 'n', 'v', 'r', 'w'

or c (s), g (j)

use '__el__' or '__al__'

le, el or al?

bottle   little   table   grumble   candle

middle   trifle   sniffle   giggle   angle

pickle   ankle   apple   simple   puzzle

camel   tunnel   travel   towel   parcel

animal   final   oval   central   signal

ss or ce?

*For the sound (**s**) at the end of a word.....*

*after **one short vowel** use* **'ss'**

*after **a long vowel***
*after **'n'*** $\Big\}$ *use* **'ce'**

ss or ce?

miss   *pass*   *chess*   *fuss*   *loss*

mice   *pace*   *choice*   *reduce*

mince   *prance*   *chance*   *pounce*

Doubling Letters.......

In a word that ends with

one vowel   &   one consonant
h<u>op</u>   sk<u>ip</u>

double *the final consonant*
before adding a vowel suffix

Doubling Letters.......

h<u>op</u>   hopping

r<u>un</u>   runner

sl<u>ip</u>   slipped

BUT

land	landing
look	looked
sing	singer
ship	shipment

Drop final e
before adding a
vowel suffix

Dropping Letters.......

hope + ing = hoping
hope + ed = hoped
but hope + ful = hopeful
hope + less = hopeless

pave + ing = paving
but pave + ment = pavement

Changing letters.......

Change final **y** to **i**
before a **suffix**

Changing letters.......

silly	silliness	sillier
happy	happiness	happily
carry	carried	carrier

BUT NOT

* if the suffix **starts with i**

carry carrying

* if there is a **vowel before y**

play played
joy joyful

Final e ....

5 important points!

Final **e** ....

Only end a word with **e** *to:*

1. *Change a vowel sound*   S<u>a</u>m → s<u>a</u>me   n<u>o</u>t → n<u>o</u>te
2. *Change the sound of* **c** *or* **g**   change   since
3. *Stop* **v** *or* **u** *being at the end*   have   argue
4. *Stop the word looking like a plural*   horse   **not**   hors
5. *Just sometimes for no reason at all*   gone   imagine

77

Reading

Words Can .....

look **short** *but sound* **long**

area

4 letters 3 syllables

idea

Words Can .....

look **long** *but sound* **short**

straight   *8 letters   1 syllable*

through   *7 letters   1 syllable*

Words Can .....

be **long** *but* **easy to read**

> supersonic
> uninhabited
> transatlantic
> electromagnetic

Words Can .....

be **short** *but* **hard to read**

eye
calf
weigh
queue

c

c can sound like **(k)**  *cat*

or **(s)**  *cycle*

c sounds like (s) before   e, i, and y

cycle to the city centre

cycle (s)

c sounds like (k) before   <u>**everything else!**</u>

cat   cost   cup   crisp   clap

cat (k)

G

g can sound like (g)

guitar

or (j)

giraffe

g sounds like (j) before   e, i, and y

giraffe (j)

gentle **gi**ant in the **gym**

g sounds like (g) before   <u>**everything else**</u>

guitar (g)

gas **g**ot **g**ut **g**rin **g**lad

W *changes......*

w<u>a</u>	to	(ŏ)	
	was	*wash*	*want*

w<u>ar</u>	to	(or)	
	war	*warm*	*ward*

w<u>or</u>	to	(er)	
	word	*work*	*worm*

87

'o' *can sound like* (ŭ)

when it's followed by: 'n'
                                 'm'
                                 'th'
                                 've'

'o' can sound like (ŭ)

on   *won ton son month front*

oth   *other mother brother*

ove   *love glove dove above*

om   *some come woman*

ti and **ci**
can sound like **(sh)**

ti (sh)   **ci** (sh)

ti   sta<u>ti</u>on   sec<u>ti</u>on   ini<u>ti</u>al   pa<u>ti</u>ent
ambi<u>ti</u>ous   supersti<u>ti</u>ous

ci   opti<u>ci</u>an   musi<u>ci</u>an   spe<u>ci</u>al
an<u>ci</u>ent   deli<u>ci</u>ous   gra<u>ci</u>ous

ch *can sound like:*

                       (ch)   *chips*

                         (k)   *chemist*

                       (sh)   *chef*

ch **(ch)** *ch*in *ch*icken ri*ch*

ch **(k)** *ch*orus stoma*ch* a*ch*e

ch **(sh)** *ch*assis ma*ch*ine para*ch*ute

Remember

Never .....

end a word with .....

q

j	**use**	ge
u	**use**	ue
v	**use**	ve

Never .....

put **S** after **X**   ex~~s~~pect

use **q** without **U**   q **u** ick

Personal Notes and Spellings to Remember!

Personal Notes and Spellings to Remember!

Personal Notes and Spellings to Remember!

Personal Notes and Spellings to Remember!